4

LET'S GO

4th Edition

WORKBOOK

D1567759

Ritsuko Nakata

Karen Frazier

Barbara Hoskins

Penny Laporte

OXFORD

UNIVERSITY PRESS

A Read and write.

> It's going to be cold.
> I'm really excited!

> I hope not.
> Is it going to rain?

> We're going to go camping tomorrow.
> _____!

> Me, too!

> How's the weather going to be?

> _____.

> _____?

> I'm not sure.

> _____.

> Me, too!

B Read and circle.

1.
humid (hot)

2.
cool   warm

3.
foggy   hot

4.
cold   humid

C Write the questions and answers.

1.

How's the weather going to be?

It's going to be cold.

2.

How's the weather going to be?

_____.

3.

_____
_____?
_____.

4.

_____
_____?
_____.

Let's Learn

A Look and check.

	Max	Amy	Mary	Joe
a mitt	✔			
a skateboard				
a bucket				
a bat	✔			
a tennis racket				
a fishing rod				
a tennis ball				
a helmet				

Max Amy Mary Joe

B Look and write.

1.

a mitt _____

2.

_____

3.

_____

4.

_____

5.

_____

6.

_____

7.

_____

8.

_____

C Write the questions and answers.

> play baseball   play tennis   go fishing   go skateboarding
> a bucket   tennis racket   a tennis ball

1. She has a ball and a mitt. What's she going to do?
   <u>She's going to play baseball.</u>

2. He has a skateboard. What's he going to do?
   <u>He's going</u> _____.

3. He has a fishing rod and _____.
   <u>What's he</u> _____?
   _____.

4. She has a _____ and _____.
   _____?
   _____.

D What are you going to do? Match and write.

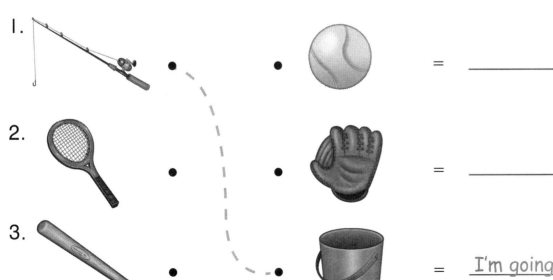

1. = _____.

2. = _____.

3. = <u>I'm going to go fishing.</u>

Let's Learn More

A Look and write.

a tent
sunglasses
a hat
a swimsuit
sunscreen
a towel
a sleeping bag
a flashlight

1. He needs a tent. _____ 2. _____

3. _____ 4. _____

5. _____ 6. _____

7. _____ 8. _____

B Read and write.

I'm going to go
to the mountains.

1. You need a tent. _____

2. _____ .

3. _____ .

4. _____ .

I'm going to go
to the beach.

1. You need sunglasses. _____

2. _____ .

3. _____ .

4. _____ .

C Look, read, and check.

1.

What do they need?
- ☑ They need a tent.
- ☐ They need swimsuits.

2.

What does she need?
- ☐ She needs a flashlight.
- ☐ She needs sunglasses.

3.

What does he need?
- ☐ He needs a towel.
- ☐ He needs a flashlight.

4.

What do they need?
- ☐ They need sleeping bags.
- ☐ They need sunscreen.

D Look and write.

1.

Does she need a flashlight?

No, she doesn't.

Does she need sunscreen?

Yes, she does.

2.

Does he need a tent?

_____.

Does he need a towel?

_____.

3.

Does she need a sleeping bag?

_____.

_____?

_____.

Let's Read

Phonics

A Match.

1.

2.

3.  • chocolate •

4.

5.

6.

• chocolate •

• sheep •

• cheese •

• shorts •

• shirt •

• chicken •

sh

ch

B Write.

1. **sh**

<u>sheep</u>

_____

_____

2. **ch**

_____

_____

C Read.

MEET **CHAD** FROM CHILE

Chile

Hola! My name is Chad. I live in Chile.

I like empanadas with chicken and cheese. I eat them for lunch. I like chocolate, too!

Tomorrow I'm going to visit my cousins. They live on a sheep farm. It's going to be hot. I need shorts and a T-shirt.

New Words
Chile
empanadas
cousins
play soccer

I'm going to play soccer with my cousins.

D Answer the questions.

1. How's the weather going to be tomorrow? _____.

2. What's Chad going to do on the farm? _____.

Unit 2 Hopes and Dreams

Let's Talk

A Read and number.

- ☐ What about you?
- ☐ Let's sing and dance together.
- 1 What do you want to be?
- ☐ I have a great idea!
- ☐ In the school show! Fantastic!
- 2 I want to be a singer.
- ☐ I want to be a dancer.
- ☐ What is it?

B Read and match.

1. a musician •

2. a news reporter •

3. a writer •

4. a scientist •

5. an astronaut •

6. a singer •

C Write the questions and answers.

1.

What do you want to be?

I want to be a singer.

2.

_____ ?

_____ .

3.

_____ ?

_____ .

4.

_____ ?

_____ .

D What about you? Write.

What do you want to be?

_____

_____ .

Let's Learn

A Look and write.

Across

1.
2.

Down

3.
4.

5.
6.

engineer   movie star   truck driver
architect   tour guide   delivery person

B Read and check.

1.

She wants to be a movie star.
☐ yes ☐ no

2.

He wants to be an architect.
☐ yes ☐ no

C Write the questions and answers.

1.

What does he want to be?

_____ .

2.

_____ ?

_____ .

3.

_____ ?

_____ .

4.

_____ ?

_____ .

D Look at C. Answer the questions.

1. Does he want to be an engineer? No, he doesn't.

2. Does she want to be a movie star? _____ .

3. Does she want to be a tour guide? _____ .

4. Does he want to be a truck driver? _____ .

Let's Learn More

A Unscramble, write, and number.

1

1. boat a sail

   sail a boat

2. a car drive

   _____

3. around world travel the

   _____

4. a mountain climb

   _____

5. a design game video

   _____

6. house build a

   _____

B Connect. Write the questions and answers.

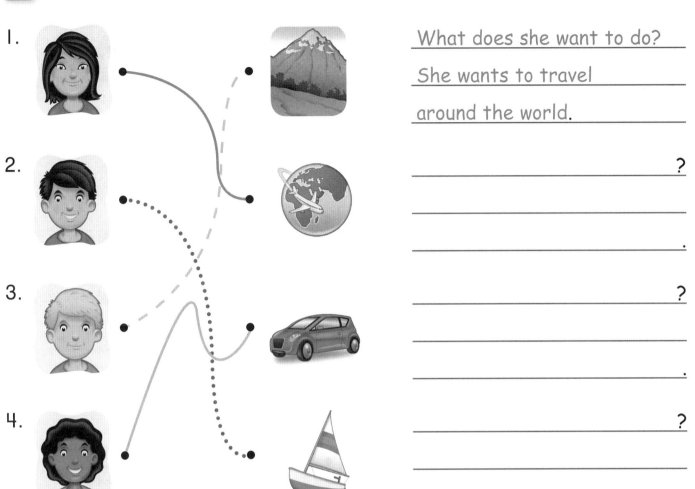

1.
<u>What does she want to do?</u>
<u>She wants to travel</u>
<u>around the world</u>.

2.
_____ ?
_____
_____ .

3.
_____ ?
_____
_____ .

4.
_____ ?
_____
_____ .

C Look at B. Read and check.

1. Does she want to build a house?

☐ Yes, she does.
☐ No, she doesn't.

2. Does he want to travel around the world?

☐ Yes, he does.
☐ No, he doesn't.

3. Does he want to climb a mountain?

☐ Yes, he does.
☐ No, he doesn't.

Let's Read

Phonics

A Match.

1. photo •

2. whale •

 **wh**

3. phone •

4. white •

 **ph**

5. dolphin •

6. whistle •

B Write.

1. **ph**

phone _____

_____

_____

2. **wh**

_____

_____

_____

C Read.

NEWS FROM HAWAII

Hawaii

Meet Anna and Teri from Hawaii

Aloha! My name is Anna. My sister and I live in Hawaii. I'm a volunteer at an aquarium. I like to watch the dolphins. They spin and flip in the air. Each one has its own whistle sound. I want to teach people about these beautiful creatures.

My sister Teri is a volunteer at the aquarium, too. She wants to be a photographer. She wants to take photos of the white whales. They swim from Canada to Hawaii in winter.

aloha = hello

New Words
volunteer
aquarium
creatures

D Answer the questions.

1. What does Anna want to do?_____.

2. What does Teri want to be?_____

Let's Review ✓

A Unscramble the questions. Write the answers.

1.  going to do What he is

_____?

_____.

2. weather How's going to be the

_____?

_____.

3.  they need What do

_____?

_____.

4. she Does drive a car want to

_____?

_____.

B Read and match.

1.    •   • She wants to be a writer.

2.    •   • He wants to be a scientist.

3.    •   He wants to travel
                                            around the world.

4.    •   She wants to design
                                            a video game.

C Read, write, and match.

| clue | beach | holding | hunt | need | sand | sunscreen | triangle |

1. "We're going to go on a treasure _____," said Aunt Angie. "We're going to take an airplane." "Yay!" said Chris and Cindy. •

• It's not a beach. But there's a lot of sand.

2. Aunt Angie had the first _____ for the treasure hunt. Chris and Cindy read it. •

•

3. Clue: It's not a _____, but there's a lot of _____. You _____ your hats and _____. Uncle Al is _____ your next clue in front of a big _____. •

•

4. "I think I know!" said Cindy. •

D Answer the questions.

1. What is Chris going to do?

   He's _____.

2. What do they need?

   _____.

3. How's the weather going to be?

   _____.

4. Does Cindy need a swimsuit?

   _____.

Unit 3 Birthdays

Let's Talk

A Read and match.

1. What's the date today? •   • That's OK.
2. When's your birthday? •   • It's the 1st. Yesterday was my birthday.
3. Oh, I'm sorry. I forgot! •   • It's on September 9th.

B Read and write.

1. Yesterday was my birthday.

   <u>I'm sorry.</u>

2. Let's have a party!

   _____

3. I forgot!

   _____

Good idea!
I'm sorry.
I forgot!
That's OK.

C Write.

1. 11th, 12th, 13th, 14th

2. 3rd, ____, 5th, ____

3. 20th, ____, ____, 23rd

4. ____, ____, 30th, 31st

5. 5th, ____, 7th, ____

6. ____, 2nd, ____, 4th

7. ____, 16th, 17th, ____

8. 24th, 25th, ____, ____

D Look and write.

| June 22nd   the 1st   Friday, June 27th   your birthday |

1. When's your birthday?

It's on _____ .

June						
Sunday	Monday	Tuesday	Wednesday	Thursday	Friday	Saturday
1	2	3	4	5	6	7
8	9	10	11	12	13	14
15	16	17	18	19	20	21
(22)	23	24	25	26	27	28
29	30					

2. When's your birthday?

It's on _____ .

June						
Sunday	Monday	Tuesday	Wednesday	Thursday	Friday	Saturday
1	2	3	4	5	6	7
8	9	10	11	12	13	14
15	16	17	18	19	20	21
22	23	24	25	26	(27)	28
29	30					

3. When's _____ ?

It's on _____ .

June						
Sunday	Monday	Tuesday	Wednesday	Thursday	Friday	Saturday
(1)	2	3	4	5	6	7
8	9	10	11	12	13	14
15	16	17	18	19	20	21
22	23	24	25	26	27	28
29	30					

Let's Learn

A Write and match.

| had | went | took | flew | slept | won |

1. _____ a party •

2. _____ late •

3. _____ a test •

4. _____ a kite •

5. _____ to the mall •

6. _____ a race •

B Write.

1. take → _took_

2. go → _____

3. sleep → _____

4. win → _____

5. fly → _____

6. have → _____

C Write the questions and answers.

1.

What did he do yesterday?

He flew a kite.

2.

What did she do yesterday?

She _____ .

3.

_____ ?

_____ .

4.

_____ ?

_____ .

5.

_____ ?

_____ .

6.

_____ ?

_____ .

D What about you? Write.

What did you do yesterday?

_____ .

Let's Learn More

A Unscramble, write, and number.

1. much too ate chocolate

   <u>ate too much chocolate</u>

2. star rock a met

   _____

3. a got present

   _____

4. money some found

   _____

5. phone lost his cell

   _____

6. broke window a

   _____

B Write.

1. eat → <u>ate</u>

2. break → _____

3. get → _____

4. lose → _____

5. find → _____

6. meet → _____

C Look and write.

What happened?

1.  **+**  **=** <u>She ate too much chocolate.</u>

2. **+**  **=** _____.

3.  **+**  **=** _____.

4.  **+**  **=** _____.

5. **+**  **=** _____.

6.  **+**  **=** _____.

D Write the questions and answers.

1.

<u>What happened?</u> _____

_____.

2.

_____?

_____.

Phonics

A Match.

• they

• Thursday

1.

third

13

• father

• thin

2.

that

THURSDAY 10

• mother

• thirteen

B Write.

1. **third**

_____

_____

_____

2. **that**

_____

_____

_____

C Read.

Meet Sama from Egypt

Egypt

Ahlan Wa Sahlan! My name is Sama, and I live in Egypt.

My brother's first birthday was on Thursday. My mother and father had a big party! They made a lot of food.

Our friends came to the party. There were two large cakes and thirteen small cakes. There were cookies and thin sandwiches, too.

We played music. Then we danced and sang. It was fun!

Ahlan Wa Sahlan = hello

New Words
Egypt
food

D Answer the questions.

1. When was Sama's brother's birthday? _____.

2. What happened at the party? _____.

Let's Talk

A Read and write.

science   best   easy   hard   like   favorite   Why   Which

1. What's your _____ subject?

2. I like science _____.

3. Really? _____ do you like science?

4. I think it's _____.

5. I don't think so. I think it's _____.

6. _____ subject do you like best?

7. I like English. It's easier than _____.

8. I _____ English, too.

B What about you? Write.

Which subject do you like best?

_____

_____

_____

C Write the words.

Down

1.

2.

3.

4.

Across

5.

6.

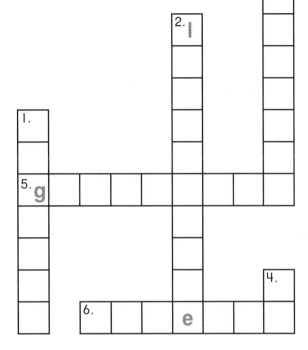

D Complete the questions and answers.

1.

What's your favorite subject?

I like literature.

2.

What's your _____?

_____.

3.

_____?

_____.

4.

_____?

_____.

Let's Learn

A Match.

1. Which sport do you like best? •

                      •

I like summer.

2. Which month do you like best? •

                      •

I like science.

3. Which season do you like best? •

                      •

I like September.

4. Which subject do you like best? •

                      •

I like skateboarding.

B Look at A. Write the sentences.

1. I like skateboarding. It's fun.

2. _____.

3. _____.

4. _____.

| It's hot.
It's easy.
It's fun.
It's cool. |

C Look and write.

rainy　hot　snowy　warm　humid　cool　windy　cloudy

1. I think _snowy_ days are better than _hot_ days.

2. I think _____ days are worse than _____ days.

snowy　　　　hot

humid　　　　windy

3. _____ _____ better than _____.

4. _____ _____ worse than _____.

cool　　　　warm

cloudy　　　　rainy

D Look at C. What about you?

I think _____.

Let's Learn More

A Match.

1.

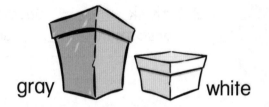

gray   white

•   • The brown bag is bigger.

2.

black   blue

•   • The black book is heavier.

3.

white   gray

•   • The white box is shorter.

4.

brown   white

•   • The white car is longer.

B Write.

1. big → ___bigger___ → ___biggest___

2. short → _____ → _____

3. light → _____ → _____

4. long → _____ → _____

5. heavy → _____ → _____

6. small → _____ → _____

C Write the questions and answers.

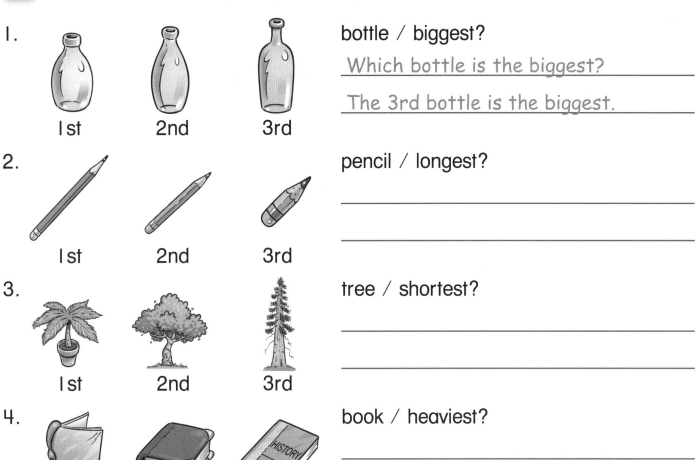

1. bottle / biggest?

   Which bottle is the biggest?

   The 3rd bottle is the biggest.

2. pencil / longest?

   _____

   _____

3. tree / shortest?

   _____

   _____

4. book / heaviest?

   _____

   _____

D Look, read, and check the answer.

1. Is the chicken lighter than the goat?

   ☐ Yes, it is. ☐ No, it isn't.

2. Is the goat heavier than the sheep?

   ☐ Yes, it is. ☐ No, it isn't.

1. Is the boy shorter than the tree?

   ☐ Yes, he is. ☐ No, he isn't.

2. Is the flower taller than the boy?

   ☐ Yes, it is. ☐ No, it isn't.

Let's Read

Phonics

A Match and write.

1.   •

2.  •

3.   •

4.  •

5.  •

6.  •

 **nk**

 **ck**

• sku_____

• du_____

• bla_____

• sti_____

• thi_____

• so_____

B Write.

1. **nk**

think

_____

_____

2. **ck**

_____

_____

_____

C Read.

ARE YOU THE FASTEST?

Are you faster than a duck? What do you think? You can run faster than a duck, but you can't fly. In the air, a duck is faster than you!

Can you swim fast? Can you swim faster than a dolphin? In the water, a dolphin is faster than you.

Can you run fast? Can you run faster than a skunk? I hope so! Skunks stink!

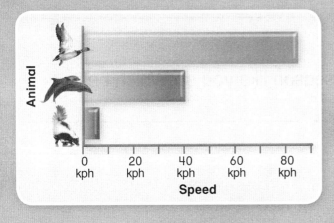

Animal

0 kph   20 kph   40 kph   60 kph   80 kph

Speed

New Words

fast → faster → the fastest
air
water

D Answer the questions.

1. Which animal is the fastest in the air?_____.

2. Which animal is the fastest in the water?_____.

Let's Review ✓

A Unscramble the questions. Write the answers.

1. did he yesterday do What

   _____ ?

   He _____ .

2. happened What

   _____ ?

   _____ .

3. What's today the date

   _____ ?

   _____ .

4. season like you do Which best

   _____ ?

   _____ .

B What about you? Write.

1. What's the date today?

   _____ .

2. When's your birthday?

   _____ .

3. Which season do you like best?

   _____ .

C Look and write.

waterfall	the Great Pyramid	kids

1. _____   2. _____   3. _____

D Read, write, and number.

☐ "This clue is _____," said Cindy.
"I _____ I know!" said Chris.

1 "Egypt is _hot_!" said Chris.
"Look!" said Cindy. "There's the _____ Pyramid!"
"And there's Uncle Al with three water bottles!"
said Chris.

☐ "Hi, _____!" he said.
"Hi, Uncle Al. Do you have our next _____?"
asked Cindy.
"Yes, I _____," he said. "Here it is."

☐ Clue: Find the _____ waterfall and ride
a _____ in front of it.

biggest
boat
clue
do
kids
Great
harder
hot
think

A Look, read, and circle.

1.

Hi, Scott. Where are you?

We're at the roller coaster.
We went on the roller coaster.

2.

Can you wait for us?

Fantastic!
Sure, but hurry!

3.

Thanks for waiting for us.

I'm sorry.
No problem!

4.

I'm so excited!

That's OK.
Me, too!

B Unscramble and write.

1.

redbo

_____

2.

sedprisur

_____

3.

deirrow

_____

4.

treesdeint

_____

5.

cixeedt

_____

6.

radasrembes

_____

C Look and write.

1.

2.

Let's Learn

A Look and write the letter.

1. up _____
2. down _____
3. around _____
4. through _____
5. over _____
6. under _____
7. into _____
8. out of _____

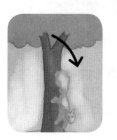
a

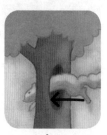
b

c

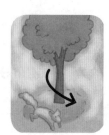
d

e

f

g

h

B Read and circle.

1. He went **into / out of** the woods.

2. They went **up / down** a hill.

3. She went **through / over** a tunnel.

4. He went **around / under** a bridge.

C Look and write.

1.

She went _____

and _____.

2.

He went _____

and _____.

3.

They went _____

and _____.

D Complete the questions and answers.

1. Where did the bird go?

The bird ____went into____ the barn.

2. Where _____ the horse _____?

The horse _____ the pond.

3. Where _____?

The cat _____ a tree.

4. _____?

The dog _____ the truck.

Let's Learn More

A Write and number.

| visited | listened | downloaded | practiced | played | watched |

1. _____ a baseball game
2. _____ to music
3. _____ their grandparents
4. _____ pictures
5. _____ the violin
6. _____ a board game

B Complete the sentences.

1.

They _____ on Sunday.

2.

_____ on Monday.

C Write the questions and answers.

on Thursday

on Saturday

on Wednesday

on Sunday

1.
What did they do <u>on Wednesday?</u>

<u>They watched</u>   .

2.
What did she do _____?

_____.

3.
_____?

_____.

4.
_____?

_____.

D What about you? Write.

1. What did you do on Tuesday?

_____.

2. What did you do on Friday?

_____.

Phonics

A Match and write.

•   •   • wa_____

1.
| lk |

•   • fir_____

• toa_____

2.
| st |

•   • mi_____

• la_____

• ta_____

B Circle the letters. Write the word.

1.

c   a   l   r
ⓣ   i   e   k

_____

2.

b   a   d   k
w   l   l   o

_____

3.

c   a   a   c
l   r   s   t

_____

C Read.

STEVE'S TRIP TO MEXICO

Mexico

Last summer, I visited Mexico.

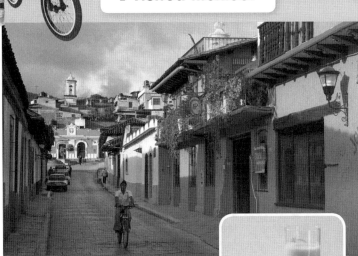

DAY 1

On the first day, we walked around an old town. I had toast and *horchata*. *Horchata* is rice milk. It was good!

DAY 2

On the second day, we hiked down a hill into a big cave. It was cold.

DAY 3

On the last day, we went to see the pyramid. We climbed to the top. It was hard.

D Answer the questions.

1. What did Steve do last summer?_____.

2. Did Steve go under the pyramid?_____.

✓ Parent's signature: _____

Let's Talk

A Look, read, and write.

Who are you looking for   Is that her
Can I help you   What does she look like

1. _____ ?

Yes, thanks. I'm looking for someone.

2. _____ ?

TRAIN

I'm looking for my aunt.

3. _____ ?

She has short red hair.

4. _____ ?

Yes, it is. Thanks!

B Read and check.

1. Is that your dad?
   - a. ☐ I'm OK.
   - b. ☐ I'm sorry.
   - c. ☐ Yes, it is.

2. Who are you looking for?
   - a. ☐ She has short hair.
   - b. ☐ I'm looking for my aunt.
   - c. ☐ Thanks!

C Look and write.

Dana

dad   mom   aunt   uncle   cousin
younger sister   grandma   grandpa

1. _uncle_ _____   2. _____

3. _____   4. _____

5. _____   6. _____

7. _____   8. _____

D Look at C. Write the questions and answers.

1.

Who are you looking for?

I'm looking for my cousin.

2.

_____?

_____.

3.

_____?

_____.

Let's Learn

A Look, read, and circle.

1.

   He has (curly) / straight hair and a beard / moustache.

2.

   She has short / curly hair and bangs / a ponytail.

3.

   He has a moustache / beard and long / straight hair.

4.

   She has curly / straight hair and a ponytail. / bangs

B Look at the chart. Circle True or False.

	Eye color	Hair style	Hair color
Joe	green	straight	brown
Paul	brown	curly	red
Liz	blue	long	blond
Tina	black	bangs	black

1. Liz has blond hair and brown eyes.
   True   False

2. Joe has green eyes and brown hair.
   True   False

3. Paul has blond hair and brown eyes.
   True   False

4. Tina has black hair and bangs.
   True   False

C Write the question or answer.

Maxine's Photos

Mom and Dad

Cousin Sal and Uncle Jim

Grandma and Grandpa

My sister and me

1. What does Maxine's mom look like?

_____.

2. What does her sister look like?

_____.

3. What does her cousin look like?

_____.

4. _____?

He has a moustache and curly hair.

5. _____?

He has gray hair and a moustache.

6. _____?

He has black hair and a beard.

Let's Learn More

A **Label the pictures. Find and circle the words.**

1.

a _vest_

2.

a _____

3.

a _____

4.

a _____

5.

a _____

6.

_____

7.

_____

8.

_____

k	e	r	s	i	e	t	m	n	q	r	s
a	g	c	f	l	v	e	s	t	o	z	n
r	l	m	g	b	a	c	p	q	l	f	e
b	a	s	e	b	a	l	l	c	a	p	a
n	s	e	a	l	b	p	s	v	i	m	k
n	s	o	t	o	h	s	h	e	t	o	e
t	e	b	s	u	i	t	w	y	u	o	r
i	s	v	e	s	s	a	n	d	a	l	s
e	a	b	g	e	t	h	e	w	f	j	k

B Write the questions.

Meg's Family

older brother younger sister Meg older sister father

1. <u>Which one is Meg's older sister?</u>

She's the one with long, straight hair and bangs.

2. _____ ?

She's the one with curly, blond hair and sneakers.

3. _____ ?

He's the one in a baseball cap and glasses.

4. _____ ?

He's the one in a vest and sandals.

C Look, read, and circle.

1. Which one is your aunt?

She's the one with | long   brown | hair.
                  short   blond

2. Which one is your cousin?

He's the one in | shorts | and | glasses |.
          sneakers   a vest

Let's Read

Phonics

A Match and write.

1.

2.

3.

4.

5.

6.

ng

nd

- si_____
- blo_____
- ba_____s
- ri_____
- ha_____
- ba_____

B Find and circle.

b	l	o	n	d	b	r	i
n	g	n	d	a	n	i	s
g	b	a	n	g	s	n	i
s	s	n	a	s	o	g	n
r	i	b	a	n	d	p	g

blond
band
bangs
ring
sing

C Read.

Emily Goes to France

Alex Goes to India

France

India

Emily is in Paris, France. There's the Eiffel Tower, but which girl is Emily? Emily is the girl with long blond hair and bangs. She is wearing a white shirt and red pants. Her hand is up. Can you find her?

Alex is in India. He is at the Taj Mahal, the famous palace. Can you find him? Alex is the young boy with short, curly brown hair. He is wearing a green T-shirt and jeans. He is singing a song with the band.

D Answer the questions.

1. Where is Alex?_____.

2. What does he look like?_____.

Let's Review

A Read and match.

1. What did you do on Sunday? •

2. Where did she go? •

3. Which one is your grandpa? •

4. Who are you looking for? •

5. What does she look like? •

• She has straight black hair.

• I'm looking for my brother.

• She went over the bridge and through the tunnel.

• He's the one in a suit and a tie.

• I listened to music.

B Look and write.

Tom, on Friday

Anna, on Thursday

1. What does Tom look like?
   He has _____, _____ hair and a _____.

2. What did he do on Friday?
   He _____.

3. What does Anna look like?
   She has _____ hair and _____.

4. What did she do on Thursday?
   She _____.

C Read and circle.

1. "Iguazu Falls is beautiful!" said Cindy.

   "But I'm $\begin{array}{c}\text{cold!"}\\\text{wet!"}\end{array}$ said Chris.

2. "Are you Chris and Cindy?" asked a man.
   "Yes, we are!"

   "Here's your $\begin{array}{c}\text{clue,"}\\\text{cave,"}\end{array}$ said the man.

3. This place is in the $\begin{array}{c}\text{beach,}\\\text{desert,}\end{array}$ but it's always $\begin{array}{c}\text{warm.}\\\text{cold.}\end{array}$

4. It's $\begin{array}{c}\text{over water}\\\text{underground}\end{array}$ and dark.

5. Find your treasure $\begin{array}{c}\text{near}\\\text{under}\end{array}$ the castle in the big room.

6. "There are $\begin{array}{c}\text{a lot of}\\\text{a few}\end{array}$ deserts in the world," said Chris.

7. "But this is a desert with a big $\begin{array}{c}\text{castle,"}\\\text{cave,"}\end{array}$ said Cindy.

A Unscramble and write.

1.

this weekend are What you going to do

_____?

I'm going to stay home.

2.

What about you?

hockey I'm play going to

_____.

3.

in a tournament I'm to play going

_____.

Wow, that sounds exciting!

4.

luck Good you I hope win

_____!

Thanks!

B Connect and write the letter.

1. play • — • a play _____

2. plant • • horseback riding _____

3. go • • softball __d__

4. see • • shopping _____

5. go • • ice hockey _____

6. play • • flowers _____

a.

b.

c.

d.

e.

f.

C Write the questions and answers.

1.

What are they going to do?

They're going to play softball.

2.

What is he _____?

_____ .

3.

_____ ?

_____ .

4.

_____ ?

_____ .

Let's Learn

A Write the answers.

1.

   Are you going to mail a letter tonight?

   Yes, I am.

2.

   Are you going to play tennis this weekend?

   No, I'm not.

3.

   Are you going to borrow some books tomorrow?

   _____.

4.

   Are you going to rent a DVD next Friday?

   _____.

5.

   Are you going to go horseback riding after school on Tuesday?

   _____.

B Look at A. Complete the calendar.

MAY

Sunday	Monday	Tuesday	Wednesday	Thursday	Friday	Saturday
4 TODAY mail a letter	5	6	7	8	9	10 go backpacking

C Read and match.

1. She's going to read a novel next week.

2. They're going to go on vacation this summer.

3. He's going to borrow some books this afternoon.

D Write the questions and answers.

1. he / go backpacking / August

When is he going to go backpacking?

He's going to go backpacking in August.

2. she / mail a letter / tomorrow

_____?

_____.

3. he / rent a DVD / tonight

_____?

_____.

A Unscramble, write, and number.

1. the _____
   srodeugrt

2. the _____ shop
   figt

3. the _____ store
   tmantdeerp

4. the _____ salon
   tubeay

5. the _____ shop
   rabreb

6. the _____
   pruekertams

B Match. Write the questions and answers.

department store   supermarket   barber shop
gift shop   drugstore   beauty salon

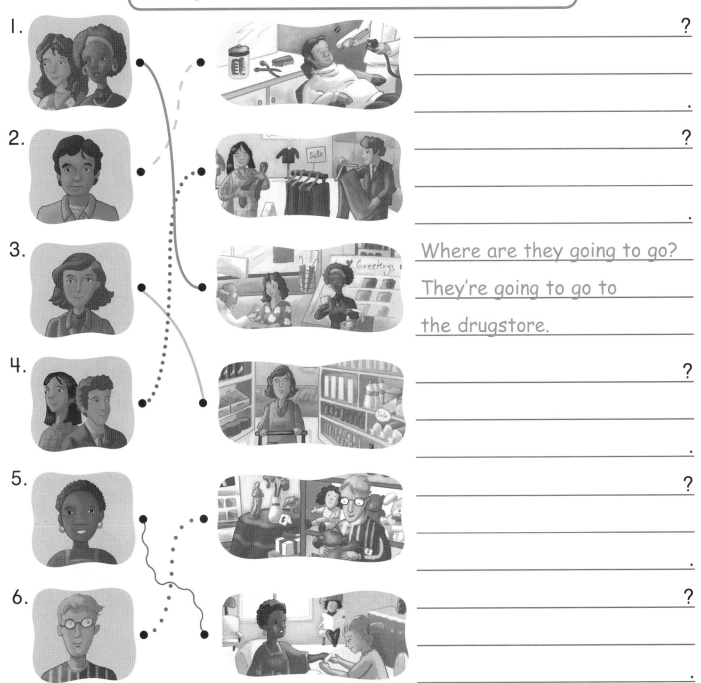

1. _____?
   _____
   _____.

2. _____?
   _____
   _____.

3. Where are they going to go?
   They're going to go to
   the drugstore.

4. _____?
   _____
   _____.

5. _____?
   _____
   _____.

6. _____?
   _____
   _____.

C What about you? Write.

Where are you going to go next Saturday? _____
_____.

Let's Read

Phonics

A Match.

1. quilt •

2. twin •

3. question •

4. twenty •

5. twelve •

6. queen •

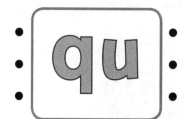

B Unscramble and write.

1. euqen = _____

2. evlwte = _____

3. liqtu = _____

4. ttenwy = _____

5. iwnt = _____

6. ntoueiqs = _____

 **Read.**

Denmark

MEET ASTRID FROM DENMARK

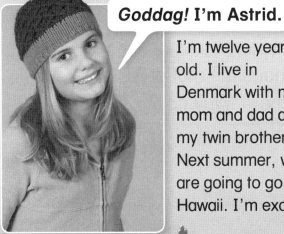

Goddag! I'm Astrid.

I'm twelve years old. I live in Denmark with my mom and dad and my twin brothers. Next summer, we are going to go to Hawaii. I'm excited.

And here is a picture of Danes with their bikes. Denmark is very flat, and Danish people love to ride bikes.

We also love to have music festivals.

I'm going to ask questions about the United States. I'm going to tell everyone about my country, too. I'm going to show a lot of photos. For example, here is a picture of our queen.

goddag = hello

New Words

Denmark
Danes
Danish
flat
festivals

D Answer the questions.

1. When is Astrid going to go to Hawaii?_____.

2. Do Danes like music?_____.

Let's Talk

A Write.

> I can't.   That's too bad.   What's the matter?
> Thanks.   Do you want to come   Why not?

1. Hi, Andy. _____ _____ to the park?

2. _____.

3. _____?

4. Because I'm sick.

5. _____?

6. I have a stomachache.

7. _____. I hope you feel better!

8. _____.

B Look and write.

Down

1.

2.

3.

4.

Across

5.

6.

7.

8.

C Look and write sentences.

1. What's the matter?

I have a _____.

2. _____?

_____.

Parent's signature: _____

Let's Learn

A Look and write sentences.

| surf the Internet | play soccer | collect baseball cards |
| watch DVDs | play badminton | send messages |

1.

She likes to surf the Internet.

2.

_____.

3.

_____.

4.

_____.

5.

_____.

6.

_____.

B Look, read, and match.

1.

2.

3.

What do you like to do?
   I like to watch TV.

What do you like to do?
   I like to play soccer.

What do you like to do?
   I like to collect baseball cards.

C Write the questions and answers.

1.

What does she like to do?

She likes to play badminton.

2.

_____?

_____.

3.

_____?

_____.

4.

_____?

_____.

Let's Learn More

A Look and write.

vacuum the carpet   take out the trash   clear the table

sweep the floor   wash the dishes   dry the dishes

1. I have to _____.

2. He has to _____.

3. She has to _____.

4. They have to _____.

5. He has to _____.

6. I have to _____.

B Write the questions and answers.

1.

What does she have to do   ?

She has to   .

2.

_____ ?

_____ .

3.

_____ ?

_____ .

4.

_____ ?

_____ .

5.

_____ ?

_____ .

C What about you? Write.

What do you have to do tonight? _____

_____ .

Let's Read

Phonics

A Match and write.

1. **nt** :
   -
   - • sma_____
   - • di_____
   - • pla_____

2. **rt** :
   -
   - • pai_____
   - • te_____
   - • ca_____

B Circle the letters. Write the word.

1.

   m t n n
   t e r t

   _____

2.

   a p r r
   c a d t

   _____

3.

   p a a n l
   c r i t t

   _____

 **Read.**

EVERYONE HAS TO DO CHORES

Sain Baina uu. I'm Manai. I'm from Mongolia.

In my family, everyone has many chores to do. I have to feed our horse every day. I carry the food in a cart. My sister has to sweep our yurt. A yurt is a big tent. In the evening, we don't have chores. We like to play games.

Manai, in Mongolia

Cantya, in Malaysia

Helo. I'm Cantya, from Malaysia.

This is my garden. We have many plants. I have to work in the garden every day. I like to work in the dirt. I also like to paint pictures of the fruit and flowers.

Mongolia

Malaysia

sain baina uu = hello
helo = hello

New Words
chores
Mongolia
Malaysia
garden
yurt

D Answer the questions.

1. What does Manai like to do?_____.

2. What does Cantya have to do?_____.

Let's Review ✓

A Read and match.

1. He's going to go horseback riding. •

2. He's going to go shopping. •

3. He's going to play softball. •

4. She's going to see a play. •

B Write the questions and answers.

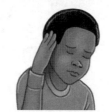

1. What's the matter?
   I have a <u>headache.</u>

2. _____ ?
   _____ .

3. _____ ?
   _____ .

C Write the answers.

1.

Where's she going to go?

_____ .

2.

Where are they going to go?

_____ .

D Write.

scrapbook
adventures
camel
Carlsbad Caverns
blank
inside
waterfall

1. "_____ _____ is so big," said Chris. "I feel so small."

2. "There's a box," said Cindy. "Let's look _____."

3. "It's a _____," said Cindy.

4. "Look! We're riding a _____ in Egypt," said Chris.

5. "And we're standing in front of a _____ at Iguazu Falls," said Cindy.

6. "Why are there _____ pages in the scrapbook?" asked Chris.

7. "Because we're going to have more _____!" said Aunt Angie.

E Read and check.

1. What happened?
   - [ ] They found a camel in the box.
   - [ ] They found a scrapbook in the box.

2. What are they going to do?
   - [ ] travel around the world
   - [ ] see a waterfall

Extra Practice

Outdoors

A **Look and write.**

1.

2.

3.

4.

5.

6.

1. It's going to be ___warm___ tomorrow.
   He's going to ___play tennis___.
2. It's going to be _____ tomorrow.
   She's going to _____.
3. It's going to be _____ tomorrow.
   She's going to _____.
4. It's going to be _____ tomorrow.
   He's going to _____.
5. It's going to be _____ tomorrow.
   She's going to _____.
6. It's going to be _____ tomorrow.
   He's going to _____.

go to the mountains
foggy
warm
do homework
cool
hot
play tennis
humid
go fishing
cold
go swimming
go to the beach

My Hopes and Dreams

A Look and write.

1. Does she want to be a writer? _____.

2. Does she want to be an astronaut? _____.

3. Does she want to be a rock star? _____.

B What about you? Write and draw.

1. What do you want to be?

2. What do you want to do?

_____

_____.

_____

_____.

Dates

A Write the numbers.

	Sunday	Monday	Tuesday	Wednesday	Thursday	Friday	Saturday
July		1st	2nd	3rd	_____	Today!	6th
	7th	_____	9th	10th	_____	12th	_____
	14th	15th	Robert's 12th Birthday	17th	18th	_____	_____
	Sarah's 18th Birthday	_____	_____	24th	25th	_____	_____
	28th	29th	_____	_____			

B Look at A. Write.

1. What's the date today? _____.

2. When's Robert's birthday? _____.

3. When's Sarah's birthday? _____.

Good Day/Bad Day

A Look and write.

1.

What happened?

I had a party and I got a present.

It was a good day.

2.

What happened?

I _____

_____.

It was a _____.

3.

What happened?

I _____

_____.

It was a _____.

B What about you? Draw and write.

What happened today?

_____.

Was it a good day or a bad day?

_____.

Feelings

A Look, read and write.

| worried | surprised | bored | excited | interested |

1.
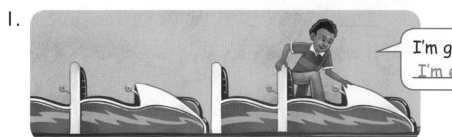
I'm going to go on a roller coaster.
I'm excited _____.

2.

I got a present.
I'm _____.

3.

I'm going to watch TV.
I'm _____.

4.

I broke a window.
_____.

5.

I'm going to download pictures.
_____.

I'm Sick!

A Write sentences.

a cold	a toothache	an earache
a cough	a stomachache	a sore throat

What's the matter?

1. He has _____.

2. _____.

3. _____.

4. _____.

5. _____.

6. _____.

My Family and Friends

A Write sentences.

Hair style	Hair color	Eye color
curly	brown	black
long	black	brown
straight	blond	blue
ponytail	red	green
bangs	gray	
moustache		
beard		

1. What do you look like?

_____.

2. What does your mother look like?

_____.

3. What does your friend look like?

_____.

4. What does your favorite singer look like?

_____.

5. What does your teacher look like?

_____.